WHAT
WOULD
ALICE
DO?

♥

"I began dealing with your house with full confidence in it in every way – and that confidence is undiminished."

*Lewis Carroll writes to
Alexander Macmillan in April, 1871*

ADVICE FOR THE MODERN WOMAN

WHAT WOULD ALiCE DO?

ATRIA BOOKS

NEW YORK   LONDON   TORONTO   SYDNEY   NEW DELHI

ATRIA
BOOKS

An Imprint of Simon & Schuster, Inc.
1230 Avenue of the Americas
New York, NY 10020

This book is a work of fiction. Any references to historical events, real people, or real places are used fictitiously. Other names, characters, places, and events are products of the author's imagination, and any resemblance to actual events or places or persons, living or dead, is entirely coincidental.

First Atria Books hardcover edition June 2018
Originally published in Great Britain in 2015 by Macmillan Children's Books, an imprint of Pan Macmillan.

ATRIA BOOKS and colophon are trademarks of Simon & Schuster, Inc.

For information about special discounts for bulk purchases, please contact Simon & Schuster Special Sales at 1-866-506-1949 or business@simonandschuster.com.

The Simon & Schuster Speakers Bureau can bring authors to your live event. For more information or to book an event contact the Simon & Schuster Speakers Bureau at 1-866-248-3049 or visit our website at www.simonspeakers.com.

Manufactured in China

10 9 8 7 6 5 4 3 2 1

ISBN 978-1-5011-9926-4
ISBN 978-1-5011-9979-0 (ebook)

FOREWORD

Where would we be without Alice? She was the very first female heroine in children's fiction; Lewis Carroll has been credited with inventing the genre itself when he created her. Just as, 150 years later, we are still following Alice down the rabbit hole, the major heroines of children's literature follow in her footsteps, from *Anne of Green Gables* to Matilda Wormwood, Hermione Granger to Lyra Bellacqua.

Alice's iconic image was created by famous artist and cartoonist John Tenniel, who was more often found lampooning politicians on the pages of *Punch* than illustrating children's books.

At first sight she appears to be a prim and proper Victorian child, every inch the little lady (little until she takes a bite from the cake marked 'Eat Me' at least . . .) but, as with everything in Wonderland, there is more to Alice than meets the eye.

Clear-headed, logical, spirited and strong, Alice consistently challenges authority. Hers is the lone, sane voice speaking out against what feminist critic Camille Paglia called the 'lunatic certitude' of the world she encounters. There is much we can learn from Alice about honesty, adventure and making your way in a world that doesn't always (ever!) make sense.

The quotes in this book are an insight into a character who is at once a hero, a window onto Victorian society and British culture, and an invitation to escape, to imagine, to play. One hundred and fifty years later, Alice still takes us in the same direction – into our own imaginations. As Carroll wrote, "I nearly forgot. You must close your eyes or you won't see anything."

LAUREN LAVERNE

ALiCE on . . .
Being Inspirational

Live your dreams

"When I used to read fairy-tales, I fancied that kind of thing never happened, and now here I am in the middle of one!"

Believe anything is possible

"Oh, how I wish I could shut up like a telescope!
I think I could, if I only knew how to begin."
For, you see, so many out-of-the-way things had
happened lately, that Alice had begun to think that
very few things indeed were really impossible.

Break the rules

"Rule Forty-two. *All persons more than a mile high to leave the court.*"
Everybody looked at Alice.
"*I'm* not a mile high," said Alice.
"You are," said the King.
"Nearly two miles high," added the Queen.
"Well, I sha'n't go, at any rate," said Alice: "besides, that's not a regular rule: you invented it just now."

Believe in yourself (and others)

Alice could not help her lips curling up into
a smile as she began: "Do you know, I always
thought Unicorns were fabulous monsters, too!
I never saw one alive before!"
"Well, now that we *have* seen each other," said the
Unicorn, "if you'll believe in me, I'll believe in you.
Is that a bargain?"

Think big

"Well, I should like to be a *little* larger, sir, if you wouldn't mind," said Alice: "three inches is such a wretched height to be."

See life as a journey

"Would you tell me, please, which way I ought to go from here?"
"That depends a good deal on where you want to get to," said the Cat.
"I don't much care where —" said Alice.
"Then it doesn't matter which way you go," said the Cat.
"— so long as I get *somewhere*," Alice added as an explanation.

ALiCE on . . .
Having a Bad Day

Accept that, some days, you just don't feel like yourself

"Dear, dear! How queer everything is to-day! And yesterday things went on just as usual. I wonder if I've been changed in the night? Let me think: *was* I the same when I got up this morning? I almost think I can remember feeling a little different. But if I'm not the same, the next question is, 'Who in the world am I?' Ah, *that's* the great puzzle!"

Try to avoid bad hair days

"Fan her head!" the Red Queen anxiously interrupted.
"She'll be feverish after so much thinking."
So they set to work and fanned her with bunches
of leaves, till she had to beg them to leave off, it
blew her hair about so.

Keep your sense of humour

"I wonder if I shall fall right *through* the earth! How funny it'll seem to come out among the people that walk with their heads downwards!"

Remember, every bad day will come to an end

"I can't stand this any longer!" she cried as she jumped up and seized the table-cloth with both hands: one good pull, and plates, dishes, guests, and candles came crashing down together in a heap on the floor.

ALiCE on . . .
Getting Ahead at Work

Aim for the top job

"How I *wish* I was one of them! I wouldn't mind being a Pawn, if only I might join – though of course I should *like* to be a Queen, best."

Manage up

Alice thought it would never do to have an argument at the very beginning of their conversation, so she smiled and said, "If your Majesty will only tell me the right way to begin, I'll do it as well as I can."

Understand the job description

"Well, this is grand!" said Alice. "I never expected I should be a Queen so soon – and I'll tell you what it is, your Majesty," she went on in a severe tone (she was always rather fond of scolding herself), "it'll never do for you to be lolling about on the grass like that! Queens have to be dignified, you know!"

Every job has its perks

 "I'm sure I'll take you with pleasure!" the Queen said. "Twopence a week, and jam every other day." Alice couldn't help laughing, as she said, "I don't want you to hire *me* – and I don't care for jam." "It's very good jam," said the Queen.

Don't accept unfair criticism

"She can't do sums a *bit*!" the Queens said together, with great emphasis.

"Can *you* do sums?" Alice said, turning suddenly on the White Queen, for she didn't like being found fault with so much.

Never get emotional in the workplace

"Consider what a great girl you are. Consider what a long way you've come to-day. Consider what o'clock it is. Consider anything, only don't cry!"

ALiCE on . . .
Dealing with
Difficult Characters

Try to keep calm

The Caterpillar was the first to speak.
"What size do you want to be?" it asked.
"Oh, I'm not particular as to size," Alice hastily replied; "only one doesn't like changing so often, you know."
"I *don't* know," said the Caterpillar.
Alice said nothing: she had never been so much contradicted in her life before, and she felt that she was losing her temper.

Speak up for yourself

"No, no!" said the Queen. "Sentence first –
verdict afterwards."
"Stuff and nonsense!" said Alice loudly. "The idea of
having the sentence first!"
"Hold your tongue!" said the Queen, turning purple.
"I wo'n't!" said Alice.

It helps to find something in common

"But I don't want to go among mad people,"
Alice remarked.
"Oh, you ca'n't help that," said the Cat: "we're all
mad here. I'm mad. You're mad."
"How do you know I'm mad?" said Alice.
"You must be," said the Cat, "or you wouldn't have
come here."

Life is not a competition

"Just so!" cried the Red Queen. "Five times as warm, *and* five times as cold – just as I'm five times as rich as you are, *and* five times as clever!" Alice sighed and gave it up.

Develop a thick skin

"Why did you call him Tortoise, if he wasn't one?"
Alice asked.
"We called him Tortoise because he taught us,"
said the Mock Turtle angrily. "Really you are very dull!"

Learn to think on your feet and be tactful

"How do you like the Queen?" said the Cat in a low voice.
"Not at all," said Alice: "she's so extremely —"
Just then she noticed that the Queen was close behind her, listening: so she went on, "— likely to win, that it's hardly worth while finishing the game." The Queen smiled and passed on.

Never criticize the person doing the catering

... the cook took the cauldron of soup off the fire, and at once set to work throwing everything within her reach at the Duchess and the baby — the fire-irons came first; then followed a shower of saucepans, plates, and dishes. The Duchess took no notice of them even when they hit her; and the baby was howling so much already, that it was quite impossible to say whether the blows hurt it or not. "Oh, *please* mind what you're doing!" cried Alice, jumping up and down in an agony of terror.
"Oh, there goes his *precious* nose!" as an unusually large saucepan flew close by it, and very nearly carried it off.

If all else fails, leave

"Really, now you ask me," said Alice, very much
confused, "I don't think —"
"Then, you shouldn't talk," said the Hatter. This
piece of rudeness was more than Alice could bear:
she got up in great disgust, and walked off . . .

ALiCE on . . .
Taking Risks

Just do it

... she had never before seen a rabbit with either a waistcoat-pocket, or a watch to take out of it, and burning with curiosity, she ran across the field after it, and was just in time to see it pop down a large rabbit-hole under the hedge. In another moment down went Alice after it, never once considering how in the world she was to get out again.

Try new things

There was no label this time with the words "DRINK ME," but nevertheless she uncorked it and put it to her lips. "I know *something* interesting is sure to happen," she said to herself, "whenever I eat or drink anything; so I'll just see what this bottle does."

ALiCE on ...
Saying What You Mean

Express yourself clearly

"Then you should say what you mean," the March Hare went on.

"I do," Alice hastily replied; "at least — at least I mean what I say — that's the same thing, you know."

"Not the same thing a bit!" said the Hatter. "Why, you might just as well say that 'I see what I eat' is the same thing as 'I eat what I see'!"

"You might just as well say," added the March Hare, "that 'I like what I get' is the same thing as 'I get what I like'!"

Choose your words with care

"When *I* use a word," Humpty Dumpty said in rather a scornful tone, "it means just what I choose it to mean — neither more nor less."

"The question is," said Alice, "whether you *can* make words mean so many different things."

Don't look for hidden meanings

"If there's no meaning in it," said the King, "that saves a world of trouble, you know, as we needn't try to find any."

Listen very carefully

"Never imagine yourself not to be otherwise than what it might appear to others that what you were or might have been was not otherwise than what you had been would have appeared to them to be otherwise."

"I think I should understand that better," Alice said very politely, "if I had it written down."

ALiCE on . . .
Minding Your Manners

Always speak clearly

"Don't grunt," said Alice; "that's not at all a proper way of expressing yourself."

Develop the art of conversation

"Speak when you're spoken to!" the Red Queen sharply interrupted her.
"But if everybody obeyed that rule," said Alice, who was always ready for a little argument, "and if you only spoke when you were spoken to, and the other person always waited for *you* to begin, you see nobody would ever say anything —"

Discourage direct questions

"Who are *you*?" said the Caterpillar.
This was not an encouraging opening for
a conversation.

Learn to take a hint

There was a long pause.

"Is that all?" Alice timidly asked.

"That's all," said Humpty Dumpty. "Good-bye."

This was rather sudden, Alice thought: but, after such a *very* strong hint that she ought to be going, she felt that it would hardly be civil to stay. So she got up, and held out her hand. "Good-bye, till we meet again!" she said as cheerfully as she could.

Be a sympathetic listener

"Well, I'd hardly finished the first verse," said the Hatter, "when the Queen jumped up and bawled out, 'He's murdering the time! Off with his head!'"
"How dreadfully savage!" exclaimed Alice.

Don't accept poor hospitality

"Have some wine," the March Hare said in an encouraging tone.

Alice looked all round the table, but there was nothing on it but tea. "I don't see any wine," she remarked.

"There isn't any," said the March Hare.

"Then it wasn't very civil of you to offer it," said Alice angrily.

ALiCE on . . .
Keeping Cool in a Crisis

See change as a positive

"Curiouser and curiouser!" cried Alice (she was so much surprised, that for the moment she quite forgot how to speak good English). "Now I'm opening out like the largest telescope that ever was! Good-bye, feet!"

Try not to make a fuss

"Well!" thought Alice to herself. "After such a fall as this, I shall think nothing of tumbling downstairs! How brave they'll all think me at home! Why, I wouldn't say anything about it, even if I fell off the top of the house!"

Come up with practical solutions

As she said these words her foot slipped, and in another moment, splash! she was up to her chin in salt water. Her first idea was that she had somehow fallen into the sea, "and in that case I can go back by railway," she said to herself.

If all else fails, deny everything

"What do you know about this business?"
the King said to Alice.
"Nothing," said Alice.
"Nothing *whatever*?" persisted the King.
"Nothing whatever," said Alice.

ALiCE on . . .
Being a Feminist

Aim for the top

"I don't want to be anybody's prisoner. I want to be a Queen."

Break through the glass ceiling

"Let's pretend the glass has got soft like gauze, so that we can get through. Why, it's turning into a sort of mist now, I declare! It'll be easy enough to get through —"

Refuse to be judged on appearance

"Your hair wants cutting," said the Hatter. He had been looking at Alice for some time with great curiosity, and this was his first speech.
"You should learn not to make personal remarks," Alice said with some severity; "it's very rude."

Claim your rightful place

The table was a large one, but the three were all crowded together at one corner of it: "No room! No room!" they cried out when they saw Alice coming.

"There's *plenty* of room!" said Alice indignantly, and she sat down in a large arm-chair at one end of the table.

Be the heroine of your own story

"There ought to be a book written about me, that there ought! And when I grow up, I'll write one . . ."

Who needs housework?

The Mock Turtle went on.
"We had the best of educations — in fact, we went to school every day —"
"*I've* been to a day-school, too," said Alice;
"you needn't be so proud as all that."
"With extras?" asked the Mock Turtle,
a little anxiously.
"Yes," said Alice, "we learned French and music."
"And washing?" said the Mock Turtle.
"Certainly not!" said Alice indignantly.

ALiCE on . . .
Health and Safety

Always read the label

. . . she had never forgotten that, if you drink much from a bottle marked "poison," it is almost certain to disagree with you, sooner or later.

Tidiness saves lives

She took down a jar from one of the shelves as she
passed: it was labelled "ORANGE MARMALADE,"
but to her great disappointment it was empty:
she did not like to drop the jar for fear of killing
somebody underneath, so managed to put it
into one of the cupboards as she fell past it.

Learn from others' mistakes

. . . she had read several nice little stories about children who had got burnt, and eaten up by wild beasts and other unpleasant things, all because they would not remember the simple rules their friends had taught them . . .

Accidents will happen

. . . she jumped up in such a hurry that she tipped over the jury-box with the edge of her skirt, upsetting all the jurymen on to the heads of the crowd below, and there they lay sprawling about, reminding her very much of a globe of goldfish she had accidentally upset the week before. "Oh, I *beg* your pardon!" she exclaimed in a tone of great dismay, and began picking them up again as quickly as she could . . .

ALiCE on ...
Enjoying Food and Drink

♥

Have your cake – and eat it

Soon her eye fell on a little glass box that was lying under the table: she opened it, and found in it a very small cake, on which the words "EAT ME" were beautifully marked in currants. "Well, I'll eat it," said Alice . . .

Keep calm and the cake will look after itself

"You don't know how to manage Looking-glass cakes," the Unicorn remarked. "Hand it round first, and cut it afterwards."

This sounded nonsense, but Alice very obediently got up, and carried the dish round, and the cake divided itself into three pieces as she did so.

When in doubt, have dessert

In the very middle of the court was a table, with a large dish of tarts upon it: they looked so good, that it made Alice quite hungry to look at them — "I wish they'd get the trial done," she thought, "and hand round the refreshments!"

Learn to bake

Here the Red Queen began again. "Can you answer useful questions?" she said. "How is bread made?"
"I know that!" Alice cried eagerly. "You take some flour —"
"Where do you pick the flower?" the White Queen asked. "In a garden, or in the hedges?"

Try new flavours

However, this bottle was NOT marked "poison," so Alice ventured to taste it, and finding it very nice (it had, in fact, a sort of mixed flavour of cherry-tart, custard, pine-apple, roast turkey, toffy, and hot buttered toast), she very soon finished it off.

Always follow the recipe

"There's certainly too much pepper in that soup!"
Alice said to herself, as well as she could for sneezing.

ALiCE on . . .
Being Brave

Stand up to bullies

"How should I know?" said Alice, surprised at her own courage. "It's no business of *mine*."
The Queen turned crimson with fury, and, after glaring at her for a moment like a wild beast, began screaming "Off with her head! Off with —"
"Nonsense!" said Alice, very loudly and decidedly, and the Queen was silent.

Speak your mind

"Who cares for *you*?" said Alice, (she had grown to her full size by this time.) "You're nothing but a pack of cards!"

Defend the weak

. . . the procession moved on, three of the soldiers remaining behind to execute the unfortunate gardeners, who ran to Alice for protection.
"You sha'n't be beheaded!" said Alice, and she put them into a large flower-pot that stood near. The three soldiers wandered about for a minute or two, looking for them, and then quietly marched off after the others.
"Are their heads off?" shouted the Queen.
"Their heads are gone, if it please your Majesty!" the soldiers shouted in reply.

Be firm with yourself

"Come, there's no use in crying like that!" said Alice
to herself, rather sharply;
"I advise you to leave off this minute!"

ALiCE on . . .
Appearances

Try not to judge by appearances

"It's a friend of mine — a Cheshire-cat," said Alice: "allow me to introduce it."

"I don't like the look of it at all," said the King.

Looks can be a sensitive subject

Humpty Dumpty was sitting with his legs
crossed . . . on the top of a high wall – such a
narrow one that Alice quite wondered how he
could keep his balance . . .
"And how exactly like an egg he is!" she said aloud,
standing with her hands ready to catch him, for she
was every moment expecting him to fall.
"It's *very* provoking," Humpty Dumpty said after
a long silence, looking away from Alice as he spoke,
"to be called an egg – *very*!"

Know when to appear (and disappear)

". . . I wish you wouldn't keep appearing and
vanishing so suddenly: you make one quite giddy."
"All right," said the Cat; and this time it vanished
quite slowly, beginning with the end of the tail,
and ending with the grin, which remained some
time after the rest of it had gone.
"Well! I've often seen a cat without a grin,"
thought Alice; "but a grin without a cat! It's
the most curious thing I ever saw in all my life!"

There's always room for improvement

"If it had grown up," she said to herself, "it would have made a dreadfully ugly child: but it makes rather a handsome pig, I think."

ALiCE on . . .
Fun and Games

Begin with an ice breaker

The Hatter opened his eyes very wide on hearing this; but all he *said* was, "Why is a raven like a writing-desk?"
"Come, we shall have some fun now!" thought Alice. "I'm glad they've begun asking riddles. I believe I can guess that," she added aloud.

Take up a challenging sport

Alice thought she had never seen such a curious croquet-ground in her life: it was all ridges and furrows: the balls were live hedgehogs, and the mallets live flamingoes, and the soldiers had to double themselves up and stand on their hands and feet, to make the arches. The chief difficulty Alice found at first was in managing her flamingo . . .

ALICE on . . .
The Value of a
Good Education

Learn your lessons

"And how many hours a day did you do lessons?"
said Alice, in a hurry to change the subject.
"Ten hours the first day," said the Mock Turtle:
"nine the next, and so on."
"What a curious plan!" exclaimed Alice.
"That's the reason they're called lessons,"
the Gryphon remarked: "because they lessen
from day to day."

Have the facts at your fingertips

"I wonder how many miles I've fallen by this time?" she said aloud. "I must be getting somewhere near the centre of the earth. Let me see: that would be four thousand miles down, I think —" (for, you see, Alice had learnt several things of this sort in her lessons in the schoolroom, and though this was not a *very* good opportunity for showing off her knowledge, as there was no one to listen to her, still it was good practice to say it over) . . .

Seek out the best teachers

"You seem very clever at explaining words, Sir," said
Alice. "Would you kindly tell me the meaning of the
poem called 'Jabberwocky'?"
"Let's hear it," said Humpty Dumpty.
"I can explain all the poems that were ever invented –
and a good many that haven't been invented just yet."

Learn a new language

"Do you know Languages?
What's the French for fiddle-de-dee?"
"Fiddle-de-dee's not English," Alice replied gravely.
"Who said it was?" said the Red Queen.
Alice thought she saw a way out of the difficulty
this time. "If you'll tell me what language
'fiddle-de-dee' is, I'll tell you the French for it!"
she exclaimed triumphantly.

Master the basics

"I couldn't afford to learn it," said the Mock Turtle with a sigh. "I only took the regular course."
"What was that?" enquired Alice.
"Reeling and Writhing, of course, to begin with," the Mock Turtle replied; "and then the different branches of Arithmetic — Ambition, Distraction, Uglification, and Derision."

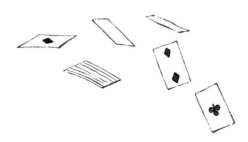

Try to keep up

"Can you do Addition?" the White Queen asked.
"What's one and one and one and one and one
and one and one and one and one and one?"
"I don't know," said Alice. "I lost count."

Learn your times tables

"Let me see: four times five is twelve, and four times six is thirteen, and four times seven is — oh dear! I shall never get to twenty at that rate!"

Use your loaf

"Can you do Division? Divide a loaf by a knife – what's the answer to that?"
"I suppose —" Alice was beginning, but the Red Queen answered for her.
"Bread-and-butter, of course."

ALiCE on . . .
Growing Up

Growing up takes time

"Oh dear! I'd nearly forgotten that I've got to grow up again! Let me see – how *is* it to be managed?"

You may experience growing pains

Just then her head struck against the roof of the hall: in fact she was now more than nine feet high . . .

Expect sudden growth spurts

"I wish you wouldn't squeeze so," said the Dormouse, who was sitting next to her.
"I can hardly breathe."
"I can't help it," said Alice very meekly: "I'm growing."
"You've no right to grow here," said the Dormouse.

When you outgrow your house, move somewhere bigger

She went on growing, and growing, and very soon had to kneel down on the floor: in another minute there was not even room for this, and she tried the effect of lying down with one elbow against the door, and the other arm curled round her head. Still she went on growing, and, as a last resource, she put one arm out of the window, and one foot up the chimney, and said to herself, "Now I can do no more, whatever happens. What *will* become of me?"

Not everyone looks their age

"Let's consider your age to begin with – how old are you?"

"I'm seven and a half exactly."

"You needn't say 'exactually'," the Queen remarked: "I can believe it without that. Now I'll give *you* something to believe. I'm just one hundred and one, five months and a day."

"I can't believe *that*!" said Alice.

Eternal youth – curse or blessing?

"But then, shall I *never* get any older than I am now? That'll be a comfort, one way – never to be an old woman – but then – always to have lessons to learn! Oh I shouldn't like *that*!"